My First...
Visit to the Hospital

First published in the UK in 2009 by
QED Publishing
A Quarto Group Company
226 City Road
London EC1V 2TT
www.qed-publishing.co.uk

A catalogue record for this book is available
from the British Library.

ISBN 978 1 84835 258 2

Author Eve Marleau
Illustrator Michael Garton
Consultants Shirley Bickler, Joanne Brougham
and Tracey Dils
Designer Elaine Wilkinson

Publisher Steve Evans
Creative Director Zeta Davies
Managing Editor Amanda Askew

Printed and bound in China

The words in **bold** are
explained in the glossary
on page 24.

My First...
Visit to the Hospital

Eve Marleau and Michael Garton

QED Publishing

Aisha and her brother Amir love to play catch with their green Frisbee.

"Hey! Over here, Amir!"

Sometimes, Amir
throws the Frisbee...

really
high,

or really wide,

or very,
very fast!

5

Amir throws the Frisbee much too high. Aisha walks backwards, her foot slips, and...

wallop!

She falls over the garden chair.

"Ow, ow!"

"My arm hurts!"
Aisha starts to cry.

7

"Mum, it hurts so much!"

"Oh dear, Aisha. Your arm
could be broken. Let's go
to the hospital to have
it checked."

8

Aisha looks worried.

"It's ok, Aisha.
The doctors at the
hospital will make
you feel better."

9

Mum and Aisha go to the **accident and emergency** waiting area to see a doctor.

There is a man with a cut on his head,

a girl with a dreadful tummy ache,

and a little boy who has hurt his knee.

"How did you hurt yourself?" asks Aisha.
"I fell over when I was playing football,"
he answers.

"Aisha Stevens!"

calls Nurse Sally. "Follow me!"

"Hello Aisha,
I'm Dr Berry.
Oh dear, what
has happened?"

"I was playing Frisbee and I fell
over and hurt my arm," says Aisha.

12

"That sounds painful! Where does it hurt?"

"Here," says Aisha.

Dr Berry gently **examines** her arm. It might be broken. We'll take an X-ray to be sure."

"What's an X-ray? Does it hurt?"

"No, it's just a special photograph of your bones."

"There's no need to be scared!" says Mum.

14

"Hello Aisha, I'm Dr Michaels. I'm going to take an X-ray of your arm."

"Put your arm on this table so I can move this camera over it."

15

Aisha and Mum go back to Dr Berry's **cubicle**.
"Right then, let's have a look shall we?"

Dr Berry turns on the light behind a big, white box on the wall, and clips Aisha's X-ray to it.

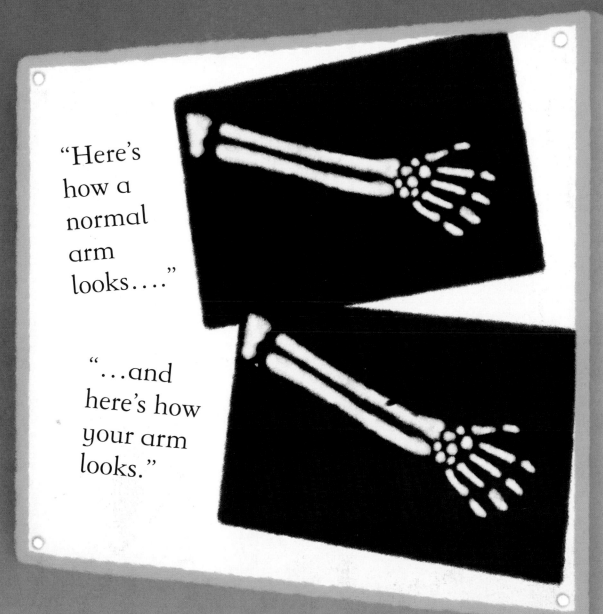

"Here's how a normal arm looks...."

"...and here's how your arm looks."

"I'll have to put a **cast** on your arm."

"What's a cast?"

"A cast holds your bones in the right position so they can **heal** properly."

18

"Would you like a blue, yellow or green cast?" asks the **plaster technician**.

"A green one, please!"

19

Dr Berry washes
Aisha's arm.

The plaster technician
prepares the cast.

Then she carefully
put the cast on
Aisha's arm.

"It might be a bit itchy, but your arm
will only take a few weeks to heal."

Aisha and Mum go home.
Aisha rushes into the kitchen.

"Amir! Look at my cast!"

"It matches our Frisbee! Does it hurt?"

"Yes, but not as much as it did."

Glossary

Accident and emergency The part of a hospital that people go to if they are hurt in an accident or suddenly feel unwell.

Cast A hard bandage that is put over a broken arm or leg to protect it.

Cubicle Part of a room that is separated off, usually used by doctors to examine people.

Examine To look at something carefully to see what is wrong.

Heal When a part of the body repairs itself and becomes healthy again.

Plaster technician Someone who makes a cast and puts it on broken bones.